Reed New Zealand Nature Series

Common Birds

in New Zealand 2

GW00703410

Reed New Zealand Nature Series

Common Birds

in New Zealand 2

Mountain, Forest and Shore Birds

Geoff Moon

REED

Cover: Kingfisher.
Title page: Silvereye.

Established in 1907, Reed Publishing (NZ) Ltd
is New Zealand's largest book publisher, with over 300 titles in print.

For details on all these books visit our website:
www.reed.co.nz

Published by Reed Books, a division of Reed Publishing (NZ) Ltd,
39 Rawene Rd, Birkenhead, Auckland 10. Associated companies, branches and
representatives throughout the world.

© 1995 Geoff Moon — text and photographs
The author asserts his moral rights in the work.

ISBN 0 7900 0370 8
First published 1995
Reprinted 1999, 2002

Printed in New Zealand

Contents

Introduction

New Zealand is blessed with a wide variety of habitats where birds live, feed and breed. These localities include our towns and cities as well as mountains, forests, wetlands (fresh water habitats), open country and coasts.

Common Birds in New Zealand 2 is the second of two volumes on the common or commonly seen birds of New Zealand. By this is meant that they are either prolific in numbers, distributed throughout many parts of the country, or that a visitor to the area in which they are most common will probably see them.

The book is not designed as a comprehensive field guide, but rather for use in practical visual identification. Colour photographs are complemented by a brief summary of information, designed more as an incentive for further interest and study than as an exhaustive reference. Scientific language has been kept to a minimum when giving descriptions and, where used, has been explained.

The species chosen for Volume 2 covering *Mountain, Forest and Shore* are not the only birds seen in these habitats, nor are these the only areas in which they are always found. Some birds, such as the Kingfisher or the Silvereye, can be seen in various habitats. However, some arbitrary decisions were required as to which volume certain species were to be placed in. Many of the introduced birds were confined to Volume 1. Volume 2 covering *Mountain, Forest and Shore* habitats records predominantly native and endemic species prominent in those parts of the country least modified by humans. Volume 3 covers the *Rare* birds of New Zealand: those rarely seen, those very small in number, and those endangered.

In some bird species sexual dimorphism occurs, where there is a marked difference in the plumage colour between the sexes. In each instance where this is evident, photographs have been included to illustrate this feature.

Taxonomists group birds into specific sections according to their anatomy. Closely related species are listed as a genus, while related genera are grouped together as a family. These families in turn are grouped to form an order. The first part of a bird's scientific name is the genus. The second name refers to the species, and the third name, where applicable, refers to the subspecies. Thus, when dealing with the North Island Robin, the order is Passeriformes (perching birds), the family is Eopsaltriidae (Australasian Robins), the genus is *Petroica,* the species is *australis* and the subspecies is *longipes.*

In this volume, the family, genus, species and subspecies are described. Common names and Maori names (where applicable) are given. The orders and families by which the birds in this volume are categorised are listed after this Introduction.

Birds are dealt with in the same order (according to anatomy) as in the *Checklist of the Birds of New Zealand,* 3rd edition, compiled by the Checklist Committee (E.G. Turbott, Convener) of the Ornithological Society of New Zealand Inc., and published in 1990 by Random Century.

Species are divided into four categories:

- *Endemic* — originating in New Zealand and confined solely to the New Zealand region, e.g. Kiwi.
- *Native* — naturally occurring in New Zealand, but also found elsewhere in the world, e.g. Blue Penguin also occurs in Southern Australia; often self-introduced from other countries.
- *Introduced* — introduced by human agency, e.g. Eastern Rosella Parakeet.
- *Migrant* — regularly migrating to New Zealand, generally for part of the non-breeding season, e.g. Eastern Bar-tailed Godwit.

Nearly all native and endemic birds in New Zealand are protected. Most are fully protected, although some, such as the Pukeko, may be hunted in their particular open season.

The size of each bird is given in centimetres, and is its length from bill tip to tail tip and, in a few instances, the length of the legs extending beyond the tail. Note that the length measurement is only a general guide to the overall size of the bird; some birds are long and thin.

I would like to acknowledge the kind assistance of the many friends who have helped me with advice, or have provided opportunities to obtain photographs.

I hope that readers find this book useful and informative, and that it stimulates further interest.

Geoff Moon

Orders and Families Represented in this Volume

Order   Apterygiformes: Kiwis
Family   Apterygidae: Kiwis

Order   Sphenisciformes: Penguins
Family   Spheniscidae: Penguins

Order   Pelecaniformes: Gannets and Cormorants
Family   Sulidae: Gannets and Boobies
              Phalacrocoracidae: Cormorants and Shags

Order   Ciconiiformes: Herons, Bitterns and Egrets
Family   Ardeidae: Herons and Bitterns
              Threskiornithidae: Spoonbills

Order   Gruiformes: Rails
Family   Rallidae: Rails and Coots

Order   Charadriiformes: Waders, Gulls and Terns
Family   Haematopodidae: Oystercatchers
              Recurvirostridae: Stilts
              Charadriidae: Dotterels and Plovers
              Scolopacidae: Sandpipers, Godwits and Curlews
              Laridae: Gulls and Terns

Order   Columbiformes: Pigeons and Doves
Family   Columbidae: Pigeons and Doves

1

North Island Brown Kiwi/Kiwi
Apteryx australis mantelli
South Island Brown Kiwi/Tokoeka
Apteryx australis australis
Stewart Island Brown Kiwi/Tokoeka
Apteryx australis lawryi

Family APTERYGIDAE
Genus *Apteryx*

Category
• Endemic.

Field Characteristics
• 50 cm.
• Females are larger and have longer bills. Stewart Island subspecies is the largest of the Brown Kiwis and often forages in daytime.
• Brown coloration with loose, coarse, bristly feathers. North Island species has darkest plumage, with dark legs. South Island species is lighter, with paler legs. The Stewart Island species also has lighter plumage but with dark legs.
• Flightless, nocturnal.

Voice
• Male utters repeated prolonged whistling calls.
• Female call is shorter and hoarser.
• Snuffling sounds when feeding.

Food
• Insects, grubs, spiders, fallen fruits.
• Probes deeply in soft soil for earthworms leaving characteristic bore marks.

Breeding
• *Time:* Throughout year, especially July to February.
• *Nest:* A burrow or depression under tree roots or hollow log.
• *Eggs:* 1 or 2 very large off-white eggs laid at intervals of 10 to 30 days. Incubation by male, but Stewart Island female reported to share incubation. Incubation period 72 to 80 days, some-times up to 90 days.
• *Chicks:* First leave burrow when 4 to 9 days old.

Distribution & Habitat
• North Island Brown Kiwi widely distributed in forested areas. High density in Northland native and exotic forests and scrubland.
• South Island Brown Kiwi con-fined to Fiordland and South Westland.
• Stewart Island Brown Kiwi confined to Stewart Island.

◀ **North Island Brown Kiwi feeding.**
◀ **North Island Brown Kiwi.**

Blue Penguin/Korora
Eudyptula minor

Family SPHENISCIDAE
Genus *Eudyptula*

Category
- Native. Also occurs in Southern Australia.

Field Characteristics
- 40 cm. The smallest species of penguin.
- Blue on back, with white undersides. On the Canterbury coast a race of blue penguins have white edges to their flippers. These 'white-flippered' penguins interbreed with normal Blue Penguins and are not now considered to be a sub-species.
- Males have heavier bills than females.
- Swims low in water and dives when disturbed.
- Comes ashore at night to roost or when nesting.
- Usually seen singly or in small groups.

◀ **Blue Penguin.**
◀ **Blue Penguin and nest in a cave.**

Voice
- Moans and a subdued quack uttered offshore before coming to land.
- During breeding season moans and high-pitched wails and screams.

Food
- Small fish and crustaceans.

Breeding
- *Time:* In north, eggs laid July to January; in south September to November.
- *Nest:* In rock crevices, caves, beneath tree roots and in burrows. The nests are often a considerable distance from shore.
- *Eggs:* 2 white eggs. Both sexes incubate for 33 to 40 days.
- *Chicks:* Fledge when 7 or 8 weeks old.

Distribution & Habitat
- Common around coastal waters from North Cape to Stewart Island.

Australasian Gannet/Takapu
Morus serrator

Category
• Native. Also occurs in Southern Australia.

Field Characteristics
• 91 cm.
• Sexes similar. Yellow head. Its large size and white wings with black trailing edges distinguish it from other seabirds.
• Dives from 20 or 30 metres, or shallow dives in surf to capture fish. Often sits on surface.
• Often seen in flocks.

Voice
• Silent except when nesting. Repeated 'awah-awah' when coming in to land. Also quacks and croaks.

Food
• Live fish captured by diving to depths of up to 15 metres in open sea. Shallow dives in surf or when catching surface fish.

Breeding
• *Time:* Early September to December.
• *Nest:* In large colonies on many islands around the coast. Mainland colonies at Cape Kidnappers, Muriwai, Pelorus Sound and Farewell Spit. Builds a mound of seaweed and grasses cemented with droppings.
• *Eggs:* One white egg. Both sexes incubate for 42 to 44 days.
• *Chicks:* Fledge at 16 weeks.

Distribution & Habitat
• Common and increasing in numbers in seas around all New Zealand coasts, especially around the North Island.
• Juveniles migrate to Australian waters and return when 4 years old to nest in New Zealand natal colonies.

◀ **Australasian Gannet.**
◀ **Australasian Gannet.**

4 Pied Shag/Karuhiruhi

Phalacrocorax varius varius

Family PHALACROCORACIDAE
Genus *Phalacrocorax*

Category
- Native. Similar sub-species in Australia.

Field Characteristics
- 81 cm. Slightly smaller than Black Shag (88 cm).
- Black with white on sides of face, neck and underparts.
- Confiding, and easily approached compared with other shag species.
- Perches on rocks or posts with wings spread to dry. Groups perch on cliffside trees.

Voice
- Silent except when nesting. Guttural croaks and gurgling sounds.

◀ **Pied Shags and nest.**
◀ **Pied Shag (Pied Cormorant) drying wings.**

Food
- Live fish, especially eels and flounder. Dives from surface.

Breeding
- *Time:* Eggs laid mainly from September to October, and another peak period in autumn.
- *Nest:* Usually nest in small colonies in cliffside trees. Trees are defoliated by these birds and often die. Nest composed of sticks.
- *Eggs:* Clutch of 3 or 4 chalky eggs is incubated by both sexes for 27 to 30 days.
- *Chicks:* Fledge when 7 or 8 weeks old, but are fed by parents for several more weeks.

Distribution & Habitat
- Frequents sheltered coastal waters, especially in northern regions.
- Occasionally seen on inland freshwater lakes.

5 Stewart Island Shag
Leucocarbo chalconotus

Family PHALACROCORACIDAE
Genus *Leucocarbo*

Category
- Endemic.

Field Characteristics
- 68 cm.
- A dimorphic species. Occurs in pied and dark-plumaged phases. Dark phase commonly called 'bronze shag'.
- White wing and black patches distinguish the pied phase from the Pied Shag.
- Displays head crests during early breeding season.

Voice
- Barks and cackles at nest sites.

Food
- Fish and crustaceans captured by diving from the surface.

Breeding
- *Time:* Nesting season varies from year to year.
- *Nest:* A very substantial nest of sticks, seaweed and other plants is built on sloping rock platforms on islets and headlands.
- *Eggs:* Clutch of 2 or 3 pale blue eggs with a chalky covering.

Distribution & Habitat
- Inhabits coastal waters from Otago Peninsula south to Stewart Island.

▼ **Stewart Island Shags, bronze and pied plumage phases.**

Spotted Shag/Parekareka
Stictocarbo punctatus punctatus

Family PHALACROCORACIDAE
Genus *Stictocarbo*

Category
• Endemic.

Field Characteristics
• 73 cm. Large and slender bodied.
• Recognised by black spots on back and prominent double head crests during the breeding season. Generally dark grey above and light grey below, with white stripe along side of head and neck. Green skin around eye. Immature coloration is all grey head and underparts.

Voice
• Grunts and guttural sounds when nesting, otherwise silent.

Food
• Dives from surface for variety of fish and crustaceans.
• Often ranges far out to sea to fish.

Breeding
• *Time:* An early nester: June.
• *Nest:* Made of sticks and weeds, built in caves or on rock ledges, often on steep cliff faces.
• *Eggs:* Clutch of 2 or 3 eggs, pale blue with a chalky covering. Both sexes incubate for 28 to 30 days.

Distribution & Habitat
• Common in coastal waters of Hauraki Gulf and Auckland's west coast.
• Also found in Wellington Harbour, Marlborough Sounds, Banks Peninsula and Otago Peninsula.

▼ **Spotted Shags.**

7 White-faced Heron
Ardea novaehollandiae novaehollandiae

Family ARDEIDAE
Genus *Ardea*

Category
- Native. Self-introduced from Australia, rare till 1940s.

Field Characteristics
- 66 cm. Slimmer than marine Reef Heron.
- Prominent white face, light blue-grey body, and dark trailing edge to wings in flight. Immature coloration: generally similar to adult, but with indistinct white face.
- Slow, leisurely wingbeat. Neck folded in flight.
- Often occur in large flocks during winter, especially on mud flats.
- Often perches on trees and fence posts.

Voice
- Guttural croaks.

◀ **White-faced Heron in flight.**
◀ **White-faced Heron, poised for fishing.**

Food
- Wide range of small fish, crustaceans, frogs, tadpoles, earthworms and insects (dragonflies, grasshoppers, blowflies, etc).
- Has habit of raking with foot to disturb invertebrates in tidal pools.

Breeding
- *Time:* As early as June or July in northern districts until January.
- *Nest:* of sticks, often flimsy, favourite site is in pine trees, macrocarpa or large pohutukawa trees.
- *Eggs:* 2 to 4 pale turquoise-coloured eggs. Both sexes incubate for 24 to 26 days.
- *Chicks:* fledge when 6 weeks old.

Distribution & Habitat
- Most common heron, now widespread throughout New Zealand on sheltered sea coasts, estuaries, harbours, inland lakes and open farmland.

White Heron/Kotuku
Egretta alba modesta

Family ARDEIDAE
Genus *Egretta*

Category
- Native. A cosmopolitan species, also in Australia and closely related sub-species occur throughout the world.

Field Characteristics
- 91 cm. Largest of the heron species.
- White plumage, yellow bill and black legs. During breeding season adults grow long nuptial plumes and their yellow bills turn black.
- As with other herons, the neck is folded back in flight.
- Slow, leisurely wingbeat.

Voice
- Guttural sounds and croaks when nesting, otherwise silent.

◀ **White Heron.**
◀ **White Heron.**
▼ **Pair of White Herons at nest.**

Food
- Small fish, eels, frogs, tadpoles and crustaceans.

Breeding
- *Time:* Eggs laid from late September to November.
- *Nest:* The only New Zealand nesting site is on the banks of the Waitangiroto River in Westland. Here, a colony of 47 pairs (1990) build nests of twigs in low trees.
- *Eggs:* A clutch of 2 to 5 pale-blue eggs. Both sexes incubate for 24 to 26 days.
- *Chicks:* Fledge when 6 weeks old.

Distribution & Habitat
- Less than 200 birds live in New Zealand. Inhabit wetlands, open country with streams, tidal lagoons.

▲ Reef Heron.　　　▼ Reef Herons.

9   Reef Heron/Matuku moana
Egretta sacra sacra

Family ARDEIDAE
Genus *Egretta*

Category
- Native. Also Asia, Australia and Southwest Pacific.

Field Characteristics
- 66 cm. Build more stocky and bill heavier than White-faced Heron.
- Recognised by its overall slate-grey colour.
- Neck retracted in flight. Slow, leisurely wingbeat.
- Spreads its wings and has a crouched posture when fishing.
- Normally seen singly or in pairs.

Voice
- Guttural croaks when disturbed or at nest.

Food
- Small fish, crustaceans and mud crabs.

Breeding
- *Time:* Eggs are laid from September to January.
- *Nest:* Built of sticks on rock ledges in caves or rock crevices, also in clumps of flax or in hollows under roots of coastal pohutukawa trees. A nest is often added to and used year after year.
- *Eggs:* 2 or 3 pale turquoise-coloured eggs. Both sexes incubate for 25 to 27 days.

Distribution & Habitat
- Throughout New Zealand. Commoner in northern North Island. Numbers decreasing.
- Frequents rocky shores and tidal inlets. Only rarely seen in freshwater habitats.

▼ **Reef Heron feeding chick at nest in a cave.**

▼ **Reef Heron fishing with spread wing attitude.**

Royal Spoonbill/Kotuku ngutu-papa
Platalea regia

Family THRESKIORNITHIDAE
Genus *Platalea*

Category
- Native. Self-introduced since 1850s.
- Also in Australia and New Guinea.

Field Characteristics
- 78 cm.
- Recognised by large size, white plumage and black, spoon-shaped bill. Black legs.
- Unlike herons, the Royal Spoonbill flies with neck extended.
- Often flies and soars in wide arcs.

Voice
- Bill clapping and low grunts when nesting, otherwise silent.

Food
- Feeds in shallow water, swinging bill from side to side to capture small fish and crustaceans.

◀ **Royal Spoonbill greeting mate.**
◀ **Royal Spoonbills fly with necks outstretched, unlike herons.**

Breeding
- *Time:* Eggs laid October to December.
- *Nest:* A few pairs nest high in kahikatea trees near the White Heron colony in Westland. Others nest on the ground on small, low islands in the Vernon Lagoons in Marlborough. Recently some have nested on Maukiekie Island, Otago, and on Green Island near Dunedin. A bulky nest of sticks is lined with grasses.
- *Eggs:* 2 to 4 whitish eggs with brown speckles. Both sexes incubate for 22 to 25 days.
- *Chicks:* Fly when 7 weeks old.

Distribution & Habitat
- Seen throughout New Zealand. Many non-breeding juveniles inhabit the Vernon Lagoons in Marlborough, the Manukau Harbour and the Manawatu River estuary throughout the year.
- Usually seen in small groups feeding at water's edge in lagoons, tidal estuaries and mudflats.

North Island Weka
Gallirallus australis greyi
Western Weka
Gallirallus australis australis
Stewart Island Weka
Gallirallus australis scotti

Family RALLIDAE
Genus *Gallirallus*

Category
- Endemic.

Field Characteristics
- 53 cm.
- North Island sub-species has reddish brown plumage, grey undersides. Western and Stewart Island sub-species are dimorphic, with dark-plumaged forms being common in Fiordland.
- Flightless; have a measured walk with a flicking tail.
- Swim well and have a strong homing instinct.
- Quite inquisitive.

Voice
- A repeated drawn out 'ee-wee' with a rising inflection.

Food
- Eats a wide range of invertebrates, seeds, fruit and lizards.
- Also robs eggs and young from ground-nesting birds and petrel burrows, and has been reported as taking mice and rats.

Breeding
- *Time:* Throughout year, peak period September to November.
- *Nest:* of dry grasses in hollow under logs or rocks, or in thick vegetation.
- *Eggs:* 2 to 5 cream-coloured eggs with dark brown blotches. Incubation by both parents for 25 or 26 days.

Distribution & Habitat
- North Island Wekas are found in Northland, Poverty Bay and on Kapiti Island. Western Wekas inhabit Marlborough, Nelson, Westland and Fiordland. The Stewart Island sub-species was introduced to Kapiti Island.
- Wekas inhabit a wide range of habitats: open country with scrub, forest margins, sand dunes and rocky shores.

◀ **North Island Weka.**
◀ **Western Weka.**

▲ South Island Pied Oystercatcher and nest on riverbed.

South Island Pied Oystercatcher/Torea
Haematopus ostralegus finschi

Family HAEMATOPODIDAE
Genus *Haematopus*

Category
- Native. Similar sub-species in Australia, South America and Northern Hemisphere.

Field Characteristics
- 46 cm.
- Black upper plumage with white below. Uniform pied marking and slimmer build distinguish it from larger Variable Oystercatcher.
- Broad white wing and back stripe visible when in flight.
- Usually seen in flocks of several thousand birds resting on shell banks and sandspits at high tide.

Voice
- Musical high-pitched 'tu-eep'.
- In breeding season a repeated rippling 'ku-vee-ku-vee-ku-vee', ending in quieter notes.

Food
- Marine crustaceans, molluscs, bivalves, marine worms and occasionally small fish.
- On farmland the birds feed on insects and other invertebrates and earthworms.

Breeding
- Thought to pair for life.
- *Time:* Eggs laid from August to November.
- *Nest:* Until a recent report from Hawke's Bay it was believed they nested only on South Island riverbeds, pastures and ploughed land. Nest is a scrape in ground.
- *Eggs:* 2 or 3 buff-coloured eggs with brown blotches. Both sexes incubate for 24 to 27 days.

Distribution & Habitat
- Throughout the year non-breeding birds inhabit estuaries, mudflats and sheltered beaches throughout New Zealand. In autumn and winter these are joined by birds which have bred, forming very large flocks.
- During the breeding season birds inhabit South Island farmland, riverbeds and sub-alpine regions.

◀ **South Island Pied Oystercatcher.**

▲ Pair of Variable Oystercatchers at nest.

Variable Oystercatcher/Torea/ Torea pango (dark phase)
Haematopus unicolour

Family HAEMATOPODIDAE
Genus *Haematopus*

Category
- Endemic.

Field Characteristics
- 48 cm.
- A polymorphic species, occurring in black, pied and intermediate phases. Only black birds occur in Stewart Island.
- Narrow white wing stripe.
- Usually observed in pairs, but flocks of 50 or more birds seen in winter months.

Voice
- Musical high-pitched 'tu-eep'. During courtship utters repeated rippling 'ku-vee'.

◀ **Pied plumage phase of Variable Oystercatcher.**
▼ **Variable Oystercatchers.**

Food
- Marine crustaceans, worms and bivalves, especially tuatua, which are placed on end in sand and prised open.

Breeding
- *Time:* October to January.
- *Nest:* A scrape in sand, on dunes or near driftwood. On rocky coasts, often sited on rock ledge or in sand between rocks.
- *Eggs:* 2 or 3 large buff-coloured eggs, marked with dark brown, incubated by both sexes for 27 or 28 days.

Distribution & Habitat
- Inhabits rocky shores and sandy ocean beaches throughout New Zealand.
- Unlike S.I. Pied Oystercatcher, it is not seen inland.

▲ Australasian Pied Stilt and nest.
▼ Australasian Pied Stilt.

Australasian Pied Stilt/Poaka
Himantopus himantopus leucocephalus

Family RECURVIROSTRIDAE
Genus *Himantopus*

Category
• Native. Occurs throughout world in temperate and tropical regions.

Field Characteristics
• 38 cm.
• Black and white plumage, long spindly pink legs.
• Distinguished from Pied Oystercatcher by smaller body, black bill and very long legs which extend well behind tail when flying.
• Increasing in numbers, and often seen in large flocks.

Voice
• A repeated high-pitched 'yep-yep'.

Food
• In marine habitats, crustaceans and molluscs. In fresh water or farmlands, prey is insects and earthworms.

Breeding
• *Time:* In wet paddocks nesting starts in July or August. In sand dunes or shellbanks nesting extends from September to December.
• *Nest:* In loose colonies, with nests formed 10 metres or more apart. Nest is a scrape in the ground lined with varying amounts of nesting material.
• *Eggs:* 2 to 4 brown eggs, heavily marked with dark-brown or black blotches. Incubated by both sexes for 24 to 26 days.

Distribution & Habitat
• Throughout North and South Island. Rare on Stewart Island.
• Occupies a wide range of habitats: wet open pastures, wetlands, lagoons, estuaries and mudflats.

▼ **Pied Stilts in flight.**

▲ New Zealand Dotterel, summer plumage.
▼ New Zealand Dotterel, breeding plumage.

New Zealand Dotterel/Tuturiwhatu
Charadrius obscurus

Family CHARADRIIDAE
Genus *Charadrius*

Category
• Endemic.

Field Characteristics
• 27 cm. Larger and stands higher than Banded Dotterel.
• Winter plumage is light grey above, whitish grey below with touch of russet on breast. Extended russet-coloured breast in breeding plumage.
• Well camouflaged when seen on sandy beaches. Call is often heard before bird is sighted.
• Runs rapidly and circles when flying.

Voice
• Call is a single 'prip', and a high-pitched 'pweep' when disturbed.

Food
• Crustaceans, molluscs and worms. On sand dunes takes sandhoppers and insects.

Breeding
• *Time:* August to December.
• *Nest:* On sand dunes or near pieces of driftwood on beach. Nest is a scrape in sand, sometimes lined with a little dry grass, is often found under pingao or marram grass, also on shellbanks. In Stewart Island, sited on rocky highlands.
• *Eggs:* A clutch of 2 or 3 buff-coloured eggs with dark-brown blotches. Incubation, mainly by female, takes 28 to 30 days.

Distribution & Habitat
• Occurs north of eastern Bay of Plenty and Raglan, also in Stewart Island. In winter some birds move to Farewell Spit.
• Prefers sandy beaches.

▼ **New Zealand Dotterel on nest.**

16 Banded Dotterel/Tuturiwhatu

Charadrius bicinctus bicinctus

Family CHARADRIIDAE
Genus *Charadrius*

Category
• Endemic.

Field Characteristics
• 18 cm. Shortish tail.
• Light brown upper parts and white below, with dark brown band around throat and russet band on chest. Male has black forehead above white stripe at base of beak.
• After nesting and moult, birds congregate to feed in flocks. Their double breast-bands are then absent.
• Runs rapidly. Bobbing movements when stopped. In flight narrow white wing stripe is visible.

Voice
• A high-pitched 'pit-pit' and a vibrating 'churr'.

▼ **Pair of Banded Dotterels at nest on river bed.**

Food
• Insects, small crustaceans and molluscs; earthworms when feeding on farm paddocks.

Breeding
• *Time:* August to December.
• *Nest:* A scrape in soil or shingle with little or no nest material. Also nests on sand dunes.
• *Eggs:* 3 brown or grey eggs with dark-brown blotches. Both sexes incubate for 26 or 27 days.

Distribution & Habitat
• Our commonest plover. Inhabits sandy beaches, mudflats, salt marshes, open short-grass paddocks, riverbeds and high country, e.g. Rangipo Desert, throughout New Zealand.
• Many birds migrate to Australia in autumn when others move to coastal estuaries.

Black-fronted Dotterel
Charadrius melanops

Family CHARADRIIDAE
Genus *Charadrius*

Category
• Native. Self-introduced from Australia in 1950s.

Field Characteristics
• 18 cm. Smaller than Banded Dotterel.
• Browny rust above, white below. Black stripe through eye and broad black V on chest. Chestnut brown patch on shoulder. Red beak. White wing patch seen in flight.
• Well camouflaged on shingle riverbeds when it turns its back to intruder.
• Undulating flight.

Voice
• A repeated 'pit-pit' and a rippling 'cree-ee'.

Food
• Invertebrates and earthworms.

Breeding
• *Time:* Eggs laid from September to February.
• *Nest:* A mere scrape among river shingle.
• *Eggs:* Clutch of 3 or 4 buff-coloured eggs with dark blotches. Both sexes incubate for 25 or 26 days.

Distribution & Habitat
• Now established on rivers of Hawke's Bay, Wairarapa and Manawatu. In South Island have colonised rivers in Marlborough, Canterbury, Otago and Southland.

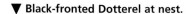

▼ **Black-fronted Dotterel at nest.**

◀ Wrybill.
▼ Wrybills.

Wrybill/Ngutuparore
Anarhynchus frontalis

Family CHARADRIIDAE
Genus *Anarhynchus*

Category
• Endemic.

Field Characteristics
• 20 cm.
• Light grey plumage above, white below. Black throat band in breeding plumage only. Well camouflaged against river shingle.
• Easily recognised by its unique bill with its tip bent to right.
• Runs rapidly.
• Very easily approached when in flocks. Flocks fly in tight formation, twisting and turning.

Voice
• A subdued chattering in flocks, a 'sweet' call in flight.

Food
• Insects, their larvae, spiders.

▼ **Wrybills.**

• On mudflats it has distinctive feeding method of swinging bill sideways to capture marine organisms from ooze.

Breeding
• *Time:* Eggs laid August to October. Late nest may be built in December if early nests lost through flooding.
• *Nest:* On shingle riverbeds in Canterbury and Otago, nest is a scrape between river stones.
• *Eggs:* A clutch of 2 pale-grey eggs with dark spots. Both sexes incubate for 29 or 30 days.

Distribution & Habitat
• In nesting season most birds move to the shingle riverbeds of Canterbury and Otago.
• After nesting, most spend autumn and winter on North Island mudflats and estuaries.

19 Turnstone
Arenaria interpres

Family CHARADRIIDAE
Genus *Arenaria*

Category
- Migrant. Occur in circumpolar region of sub-arctic. Arrive late September from Siberia and Alaska. Leave in late March.

Field Characteristics
- 23 cm.
- Tortoiseshell plumage colour and short legs distinguish the Turnstone from other migrant waders.
- White lower back and wing bar visible in flight.
- Flocks often fly off very suddenly when approached.

Voice
- A vibrating 'tit-tit' when flushed.

Food
- Insects and crustaceans.

Breeding
- Nests in tundra regions of Alaska and Siberia.

Distribution & Habitat
- Usually seen in small flocks resting on shellbanks at high tide or feeding on rock platforms.
- On mudflats and stony beaches this species turns over seaweed and stones in search of prey.

▼ Turnstones.

Lesser Knot/Huahou
Calidris canutus canutus

Family SCOLOPACIDAE
Genus *Calidris*

Category
- Migrant. Arrives from Northern Hemisphere late September. Starts on return migration late March.
- Some non-breeding birds over-winter in New Zealand.

Field Characteristics
- 25 cm. Half size of Godwit and shorter bill and legs.
- Eclipse plumage is light brown above, whitish brown below. Nuptial plumage is darker brown above, russet below.

Voice
- Muted chattering when roosting.

Food
- Crustaceans, molluscs and marine worms.

Breeding
- Nests in tundra regions of Siberia.

Distribution & Habitat
- After the Godwit this is our second most numerous wader. Inhabits mudflats, estuaries and sandspits, often in association with Godwits.

▼ **Lesser Knot, eclipse plumage.**

▲ Eastern Bar-tailed Godwit, nuptial plumage.
▼ Eastern Bar-tailed Godwit, eclipse plumage.

Eastern Bar-tailed Godwit/Kuaka
Limosa lapponica baueri

Family SCOLOPACIDAE
Genus *Limosa*

Category
- Migrant. Up to 100,000 Godwits migrate to New Zealand from Eastern Siberia and Alaska, arriving late September and returning in late March or early April.
- Some immature birds over-winter in northern New Zealand.

Field Characteristics
- 40 cm. Females are larger and have longer bills.
- Eclipse plumage is mottled greyish buff above, lighter below. Males assume russet-coloured nuptial plumage before return migration.
- Long black slender legs. Long, slightly upturned bill.
- A small number of Black-tailed Godwits, *Limosa limosa,* are seen among flocks of Bar-tailed Godwits. These can be recognised by their straighter bills, more uniform colouring, and white wing-bar and white upper-tail band in flight.

Voice
- A twittering double 'tuu-tuu' note in roosting flocks, also 'kwit-kwit' in flight.

Food
- Probe deeply in mud for wide range of marine worms, crustaceans and molluscs.

Breeding
- Nest in Eastern Siberia and Alaska.

Distribution & Habitat
- Inhabit mudflats, estuaries and coastal lagoons throughout New Zealand, but greatest concentrations are at Farewell Spit and in northern harbours.

▼ **Eastern Bar-tailed Godwits in flight.**

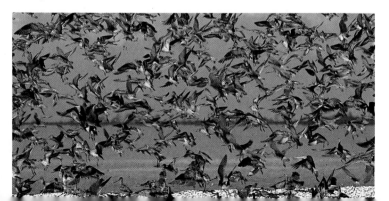

▲ Southern Black-backed Gull.
▼ Southern Black-backed Gull and nest.

Southern Black-backed Gull/Karoro
Larus dominicanus dominicanus

Family LARIDAE
Genus *Larus*

Category
- Native. Occurs in southern temperate to sub-antarctic regions.

Field Characteristics
- 60 cm. Our largest gull.
- Only gull in New Zealand with a black back. Young in their first year are brown. In second year back is brown, breast and neck white flecked with brown.

Voice
- When disturbed near territory, circles, uttering 'ga-ga-ga'. Also has long 'garw-w-w' call.

Food
- A wide range of shellfish, crustaceans, molluscs, worms and insects. Shellfish are often carried high in air and dropped to break shell. Also eat carrion.

Breeding
- *Time:* Late October to December.
- *Nest:* Most pairs nest in colonies near seashore, but others nest in isolation on rocky headlands, islets or inland near lakes, also on mountainsides at high altitudes. Nest is composed of grasses, dry seaweed and other dry vegetation.
- *Eggs:* 2 or 3 brownish or grey eggs, dark blotches. Both sexes incubate for 25 to 26 days.

Distribution & Habitat
- Common throughout New Zealand on open coasts, harbours and estuaries, also inland and often at high altitudes.
- Numerous at city refuse dumps.

▼ **Southern Black-backed Gull on left with immature bird.**

Red-billed Gull/Tarapunga
Larus novaehollandiae scopulinus

Family LARIDAE
Genus *Larus*

Category
- Native. Also occur in Australia and South Africa.

Field Characteristics
- 37 cm. Heavier build, thicker bill than Black-billed Gull.
- Adults easily recognised: white body, pearly grey back, black wing feathers with white tips. Short red legs, red feet and eye ring. Juveniles have brown tips to feathers of back and mantle, dark-brown bill and legs.

Voice
- High-pitched, raucous 'scrark'.

Food
- Small fish, crustaceans and molluscs.
- Paddle with feet in wet sand to bring up worms.
- In flooded paddocks they eat earthworms and insects.
- Also rob eggs from White-fronted Terns' nests.

Breeding
- Sometimes interbreed with Black-billed Gulls.
- *Time:* September to December.
- *Nest:* In colonies on rocky headlands and islets off coast. A few pairs nest inland with Black-billed Gulls on shore of Lake Rotorua. Nests, close together, are composed of dry grasses and seaweed.
- *Eggs:* 2 brown-coloured heavily blotched eggs. Both sexes incubate for 24 to 26 days.

Distribution & Habitat
- Common throughout New Zealand around coasts, estuaries, and urban parks, but uncommon inland.

▼ **Red-billed Gull.**

Black-billed Gull
Larus bulleri

Family LARIDAE
Genus *Larus*

Category
- Endemic.

Field Characteristics
- 37 cm. Slimmer build than Red-billed Gull.
- Similar colouring to Red-billed Gull but with noticeably thinner black bill and legs.
- Less confiding to humans than Red-billed Gull.

Voice
- Similar to Red-billed Gull but quieter.

Food
- Insects and their larvae, invertebrates and earthworms. Often follow plough.
- On coast eat crustaceans and molluscs.

Breeding
- *Time:* Eggs laid October to December.
- *Nest:* Usually nest on inland riverbeds and shores of some lakes. Most nest in South Island. Some small colonies are found on sheltered coastal spits of North and South Island. The nest is often quite substantial, composed of small sticks and grasses.
- *Eggs:* Clutch of 2 brown, heavily blotched eggs. Both sexes incubate for 22 to 24 days.

Distribution & Habitat
- Inhabits inland lakes, rivers and estuaries. Tends to migrate to coasts in winter months. More common in South Island.

▼ **Black-billed Gull.**

▲ Black-fronted Tern.
▼ Black-fronted Tern and nest on riverbed.

Black-fronted Tern/Tarapiroe
Sterna albostriata

Family LARIDAE
Genus *Sterna*

Category
- Native. Similar sub-species occur in Australia, Europe, South Asia and Africa.

Field Characteristics
- 30 cm. Noticeably smaller than White-fronted Tern.
- Grey plumage, darker than White-fronted Tern. Orange-coloured bill and feet. Black crown becomes grey and mottled after post-nuptial moult.
- White rump seen in flight.

Voice
- Calls repeatedly with sharp 'tit-tit-tit' when in flight.

Food
- Small fish, insects and earthworms.

▼ **Black-fronted Tern on nest.**

- Often seen in flocks hawking insects on inland farm paddocks.

Breeding
- *Time:* Eggs laid from mid October to December.
- *Nest:* On shingle riverbeds of eastern South Island in small loose colonies, with nests (formed by a scrape in sand or shingle) 10 or more metres apart. Many nests are destroyed by flash floods or predation.
- *Eggs:* 2 or 3 grey eggs with dark-brown blotches. Incubated by both sexes for 21 to 23 days.

Distribution & Habitat
- Inhabits riverbeds and farmlands east of the Southern Alps. In autumn most birds migrate to coastal river estuaries in both South and North Islands.

▲ Caspian Terns and chick.
▼ Caspian Tern colony on an ocean beach.

Caspian Tern/Taranui
Sterna caspia

Family LARIDAE
Genus *Sterna*

Category
- Native. A cosmopolitan species, they occur throughout world in tropical and temperate zones.

Field Characteristics
- 51 cm. New Zealand's largest tern.
- Light grey above, white below, with black crown.
- Easily recognised by its heavy body and sickle-shaped wings and tail with shallow fork. On ground, its heavy red bill becomes evident.
- Black cap becomes grey and speckled after breeding season, and a slight head-crest is sometimes evident.

Voice
- A harsh, rasping 'karak'.

▼ **Caspian Tern in flight.**

Food
- Feed only on live fish caught by a splashing plunge from 8 to 10 metres above surface.

Breeding
- *Time:* September to January.
- *Nest:* In colonies on shellbanks in harbours or among sand dunes. Some pairs nest in isolation on shingle riverbeds, sandy beaches on small islands, or the shores of lakes. Nest is a mere scape in the sand.
- *Eggs:* 1 to 3 unusually large buff-coloured, dark-spotted eggs. Both sexes incubate for 21 to 23 days.

Distribution & Habitat
- North and South Islands: shallow coastal waters, estuaries, lagoons.
- Sometimes seen in small numbers on inland lakes.

White-fronted Tern/Tara
Sterna striata

Family LARIDAE
Genus *Sterna*

Category
- Endemic.

Field Characteristics
- 42 cm.
- Silver grey above, white below. Black crown. Distinguished from smaller Black-fronted Tern by general lighter plumage and black bill and feet.
- Juvenile coloration: crown mottled with brown, black striping on browny grey back and wings.
- Forked tail.
- Common name of 'kahawai bird' derived from this tern's habit of fishing over surface shoals of these fish.

Voice
- A high-pitched repeated 'zitt-zitt'.

Food
- Dives for small fish captured just below surface.

Breeding
- *Time:* October to January.
- *Nest:* In colonies on rock headlands and islets, shellbanks and sandy beaches, also on ledges of cliffs. Nests are close together.
- *Eggs:* 1 or 2 buff or grey eggs with dark spots are laid on bare ground. Incubation by both sexes for 21 days.

Distribution & Habitat
- Our commonest tern. Inhabits coastal waters throughout New Zealand. Seldom seen inland.
- Many birds migrate to Australia in autumn but do not nest there.

◀ **White-fronted Terns nesting.**
◀ **White-fronted Tern colony.**
▼ **White-fronted Tern, adult, and newly fledged chick.**

▲ New Zealand Pigeon and nest with five-day-old chick.

New Zealand Pigeon/Kereru
Hemiphaga novaeseelandiae novaeseelandiae

Family COLUMBIDAE
Genus *Hemiphaga*

Category
- Endemic.

Field Characteristics
- 51 cm.
- Identified by large size, general iridescent greyish-green colour with pure white breast. Red beak and feet.
- Heavy flight with pronounced whistling wingbeat.
- Spectacular rising and falling nuptial flights in spring.

Voice
- A subdued 'goo' or 'ooh'.

Food
- Eats a wide range of fruits, seeds, flowers and foliage of native and exotic plants.
- Important agent for dispersing seed from many plants, especially seeds from podocarp trees.

Breeding
- *Time:* Nesting extends from late August to March.
- *Nest:* A flimsy structure of small twigs loosely crossed.
- *Eggs:* The single white egg is often visible from below. Incubation by both sexes takes 29 or 30 days. Clutch overlap may occur, when chick in first nest is attended while a second egg is incubated in a new nest.

Distribution & Habitat
- Widespread throughout forested areas of New Zealand.
- Also seen in open country when feeding on broom flowers and clover.

◀ **New Zealand Pigeon feeding on nikau fruit.**
▼ **New Zealand Pigeon feeding five-week-old chick.**

North Island Kaka
Nestor meridionalis septentrionalis

Family PSITTACIDAE
Genus *Nestor*

Category
- Endemic.

Field Characteristics
- 45 cm.
- Light crown and nape. In flight shows rounded wings with scarlet and orange-coloured underwing.
- Large hooked bill.
- Often calls when flying at night.
- Some birds visit suburban gardens during winter to feed on exotic plants.

Voice
- Harsh grating call when disturbed or flying, otherwise soft melodious whistles and warbles.
- Soft low whistles and chuckles at nest.

▼ **North Island Kaka.**

Food
- Wide range of foliage, shoots, fruits, nectar, insects, larvae.
- Strong beak used to rip bark and wood from dead trees in search of grubs.

Breeding
- *Time:* November to January.
- *Nest:* In cavity of mature or dead tree. Nest material is powdered wood.
- *Eggs:* Clutch of 2 to 4 white eggs. Incubation by female, fed on the nest every $1^1/2$ hours by male. Incubation period 24 to 26 days.
- *Chicks:* Fledge when 10 weeks old, flightless for 2 or 3 days.

Distribution & Habitat
- Inhabits large tracts of lowland forest in the North Island and forested offshore islands.

South Island Kaka
Nestor meridionalis meridionalis

Family PSITTACIDAE
Genus *Nestor*

Category
• Endemic.

Field Characteristics
• 46 cm. Slightly larger than North Island sub-species.
• Greenish tinge and whitish crown. Red belly.

Voice
• Similar calls to North Island Kaka.

▼ **A captive South Island Kaka.**

Food
• Seeds, foliage, shoots, fruits, nectar, insects and grubs.

Breeding
• Not studied extensively, but considered similar to North Island Kaka.

Distribution & Habitat
• Inhabits forest from Nelson Province, West Coast, Fiordland to Stewart Island.

Kea
Nestor notabilis

Family **PSITTACIDAE**
Genus *Nestor*

Category
• Endemic.

Field Characteristics
• 46 cm.
• Olive-green plumage and large hooked beak distinguish it from South Island Kaka. Orange underwing prominent in flight.
• Confiding, inquisitive and destructive to human belongings.

Voice
• High-pitched 'kee-aa' call, especially when flying, also softer murmuring and whistling calls.

◄ The bright underwing colour of a Kea.
◄ Kea.
▼ Kea.

Food
• Seeds, foliage, fruits, insects and nectar.
• Also feeds on carrion and attacks sickly sheep.

Breeding
• Males sometimes mate with two or more females.
• *Time:* Eggs laid from August to January.
• *Nest:* Unlike other parrots, the Kea builds a nest of sticks, grasses, moss and lichens, usually under rock above the bush-line or in a forest clearing.
• *Eggs:* Clutch of 2 or 3 white eggs. Incubation period 23 to 24 days.

Distribution & Habitat
• Inhabits South Island high-country forests and mountains.

Eastern Rosella
Platycercus eximius

Family PSITTACIDAE
Genus *Platycercus*

Category
- Introduced from Eastern Australia or cage-escaped birds.

Field Characteristics
- 33 cm.
- Brilliantly coloured with red, yellow, green and white.
- Prominent long tail.
- Flight is rapid and direct.
- Seen in pairs or small groups.

Voice
- Varies with district. Northland birds call with a three-note whistle, with second note lower in pitch. Birds in other areas have a double-note call.
- Chatter when feeding.

Food
- Wide range of fruits, buds and shoots and flowers.
- Seeds of Scotch thistle.

Breeding
- *Time:* October to January.
- *Nest:* In cavities in trees, or dead tree fern trunks.
- *Eggs:* 4 to 6 white eggs, incubated by hen for 22 to 24 days.

Distribution & Habitat
- Common in Northland, Waitakeres, Coromandel, western Waikato, Wairarapa and Upper Hutt Valley. Small numbers in Canterbury, Otago and Stewart Island.
- Inhabits forest and open country close to forests.
- The Crimson Rosella, *Platycercus elegans*, another cage-escapee, occurs in small numbers in northwest Wellington.

▼ A pair of Eastern Rosella Parakeets.

Yellow-crowned Parakeet/Kakariki
Cyanoramphus auriceps auriceps

Family PSITTACIDAE
Genus *Cyanoramphus*

Category
- Endemic.

Field Characteristics
- 25 cm.
- Green plumage, with red forehead and yellow crown. Long tail.
- Usually seen in small groups, generally high in forest canopy. On offshore islands often forages on ground.

Voice
- Rapid 'ki-ki-ki' when in flight; chatters when feeding.

Food
- Seeds, buds and shoots of shrubs, fruits and flowers, invertebrates.

Breeding
- *Time:* October to January.
- *Nest:* In cavities in trees, often in end of dead, broken limbs.
- *Eggs:* Clutch of 4 to 8 white eggs, incubated for 20 days by female who is fed by male.

Distribution & Habitat
- Inhabits forested areas of central North Island and Tararua Ranges, also common on many offshore islands. In South Island widespread from Marlborough through Nelson, Westland to Fiordland, also found in parts of Canterbury, Otago and Stewart Island.
- This species is far more common on the mainland than the Red-crowned Parakeet.

▼ Yellow-crowned Parakeet.

Red-crowned Parakeet/Kakariki
Cyanoramphus novaezelandiae novaezelandiae

Family PSITTACIDAE
Genus *Cyanoramphus*

Category
- Native. Also occur in New Caledonia.

Field Characteristics
- 28 cm.
- Red forehead and crown prominent. Red patch behind eye. Usually well camouflaged when feeding in broadleaf trees.
- Flight rapid and direct.
- Often seen in groups.

Voice
- A rapid babbling chatter when feeding. Repeated 'ke-ke-ke' when flying.

◀ **Red-crowned Parakeet pair at nest hole, female feeding chick.**
▼ **Red-crowned Parakeet, male feeding female.**

Food
- Seeds, buds and shoots, flowers, fruits and nectar. Also eat invertebrates but far less than does Yellow-crowned Parakeet.

Breeding
- *Time:* Eggs laid from October to January.
- *Nest:* In cavity of trees. On some offshore islands nest in rock crevices on ground.
- *Eggs:* Clutch of 4 to 9 white eggs. Incubation for 20 days by female who is called from nest and fed by male at hourly intervals. Male also assists in feeding chicks.

Distribution & Habitat
- Inhabits lowland native forests. Common on many offshore islands, but becoming increasingly scarce on mainland.

Shining Cuckoo/Pipiwharauroa
Chrysococcyx lucidus lucidus

Family CUCULIDAE
Genus *Chrysococcyx*

Category
• Native. Migratory: winters in Solomon Islands, Bougainville and other Pacific Islands in that region. Arrives in New Zealand late September.

Field Characteristics
• 16 cm. Size of a House Sparrow.
• Iridescent green above, grey below with green bars. Female and immature: duller with less distinct bars on cheeks.
• Well camouflaged in foliage; more often heard than seen.
• Rapid flight.

Voice
• Repeated whistle, each note a rising inflection, followed by descending notes.

Food
• Insects and spiders, especially hairy caterpillars.

Breeding
• *Time:* October to January.
• Nest: Uses nests of Grey Warbler.
• *Eggs:* Lays one egg per nest, with total number unknown. Incubation 12 days.
• *Chicks:* Fed by foster parent for several weeks after fledging.

Distribution & Habitat
• Inhabits forest and open country with trees, September to February.

▼ **Shining Cuckoo.**

Long-tailed Cuckoo/Koekoea
Eudynamys taitensis

Family CUCULIDAE
Genus *Eudynamys*

Category
- Native. Migratory: winters from Bismarch Archipelago to Marquesa Islands, arrives in New Zealand October.

Field Characteristics
- 40 cm.
- Speckled brown. Female and immature: greyish brown speckled above with pale spots, undersides reddish buff with fine dark streaks.
- Hawk-like appearance. Very long tail is prominent when flying.

Voice
- A repeated harsh, hissing screech with a rising inflection. Also a metallic short alarm note.

Food
- Insects, grubs and lizards. Is predatory, robbing eggs and chicks from nests.
- Also reported to have taken small birds and mice.

Breeding
- *Time:* November to December.
- *Nest:* Lays single egg in nest of Whitehead in North Island, and Yellowhead and Brown Creeper in South Island.
- *Eggs:* Creamy white egg blotched with purplish brown and grey. 1 egg per nest of host, total number unknown.

Distribution & Habitat
- Inhabits forested regions where Whiteheads and Yellowheads live, October to February.

◀ Long-tailed Cuckoo.
▼ Long-tailed Cuckoo in flight.

▲ Morepork with weta.

Morepork/Ruru
Ninox novaeseelandiae novaeseelandiae

Family STRIGIDAE
Genus *Ninox*

Category
• Our only endemic owl.

Field Characteristics
• 29 cm.
• Dark brown above, speckled brown and rust below. Distinguished from introduced Little Owl by dark plumage, rounder head and longer tail.
• Generally nocturnal.

Voice
• Usual call of 'Quor-quo'. Also a vibrating 'cree' and short 'quee' with rising inflection.

Food
• Mainly insects, especially moths, wetas and stick insects. Also, small birds, mice, geckos.

Breeding
• *Time:* Eggs laid late October or November.
• *Nest:* In tree hollows, clumps of perching epiphytes or in fork of pine tree on bed of pine needles.
• *Eggs:* 2, occasionally 3, white eggs, incubated by female for 31 days. Female fed by male.
• *Chicks:* Fed by both parents, and fledge when $4^{1}/_{2}$ weeks old.

Distribution & Habitat
• Found throughout New Zealand but uncommon in eastern South Island.
• Essentially inhabits forests, but adapted to live in open country with clumps of trees for shelter and nesting.

◀ **Morepork flying to nest.**
▼ **Three-week-old Morepork chicks.**

▼ **Morepork at nest hole.**

▲ New Zealand Kingfisher with crab.

38 New Zealand Kingfisher/Kotare
Halcyon sancta vagans

Family ALCEDINIDAE
Genus *Halcyon*

Category
• Native. Also Australia.

Field Characteristics
• 24 cm.
• Bright greenish blue above and off-white to buff below. Male more brightly coloured than female. Russet on flanks and underwing fades in summer. Immature coloration: duller, with darker mottled breast.
• Large black pointed bill. Very short legs.
• A wary bird. Often seen perched on rocks, posts, power lines and trees as vantage points, waiting to capture prey.
• Direct flight.

Voice
• Repeated 'kek-kek-kek'.
• During courtship a vibrating 'keree-keree' with rising inflection.
• Also short 'krek' when boring holes.

◄ **New Zealand Kingfisher with fish.**

Food
• Insects and their larvae, earthworms, spiders, tadpoles, fish, crabs, freshwater crayfish, skinks, small birds and mice.

Breeding
• *Time:* Eggs laid November to January.
• *Nest:* Bores tunnels in clay banks or rotting tree trunks, or uses cavities in trees.
• *Eggs:* 4 or 5 white eggs. Incubation shared by sexes, but mainly by female.
• *Chicks:* Both parents feed chicks, which fledge when 26 days old. Fed by parents for further 10 days.

Distribution & Habitat
• Common throughout New Zealand, especially in coastal regions of the northern North Island.
• Lives in marine habitats, wetlands, open country, along water courses, farmland and forests. Migrates to coastal areas during winter months.

▲ South Island Rifleman.

South Island Rifleman/Titipounamu
Acanthisitta chloris chloris
North Island Rifleman/Titipounamu
Acanthisitta chloris granti

Family ACANTHISITTIDAE
Genus *Acanthisitta*

Category
• Endemic.

Field Characteristics
• 8 cm. New Zealand's smallest bird.
• Male is mainly green above, greenish grey below. Female is streaked buff and dark brown above.
• Recognised by short tail and brisk movements, often spiralling around tree trunks when feeding.

Voice
• A very high-pitched 'zit-zit'.

Food
• Insects, larvae and spiders.

Breeding
• *Time:* September to January.
• *Nest:* A globe of fine grasses and moss, lined with feathers, built under flaking bark, knot-hole in tree or in bank.
• *Eggs:* 3 or 4 white eggs. Both sexes incubate for 20 days.
• *Chicks:* Often fed by immature birds of previous nestings.

Distribution & Habitat
• As well as Little and Great Barrier Islands, the North Island Rifleman inhabits native and exotic forest south of Te Aroha.
• South Island Rifleman inhabits exotic and native forests throughout South Island, especially in high-altitude beech forests.

◀ **South Island Rifleman near nest hole.**
▼ **South Island Rifleman.**

▼ **North Island Rifleman.**

40 Whitehead/Popokatea
Mohoua albicilla

Family PACHYCEPHALIDAE
Genus *Mohoua*

Category
• Endemic.

Field Characteristics
• 15 cm.
• Dull brown above, head and underparts white tinged with brown. Female duller on head.
• After nesting season, move noisily around canopy of forest in small groups. Readily respond to squeaker.

Voice
• Repeated 'chip' or 'zwit' as birds move around in groups.
• Male's song is a soft, canary-like trill and whistle.

Food
• Insects and grubs from foliage and bark. Often hang upside down to feed. Also take fruits and seed.

Breeding
• Often polygamous, with 3 or 4 birds attending a nest and feeding chicks.
• *Time:* October to January.
• *Nest:* Composed of grasses, moss and lichen, is often lined with tree-fern scales and a few feathers. Built in shrub or fork of tree.
• *Eggs:* Clutch of 3 or 4 pinkish-coloured eggs. Incubated by both sexes, or often 2 females, for 17 days.

Distribution & Habitat
• Inhabits forest and scrub in the North Island. Apart from good populations on Little Barrier Island and Tiritiri Island, does not occur north of Te Aroha.

◀ **Whitehead and nest.**
▼ **Whitehead on nest in mingimingi shrub.**

Yellowhead/Mohua
Mohoua ochrocephala

Family PACHYCEPHALIDAE
Genus *Mohoua*

Category
- Endemic.

Field Characteristics
- 15 cm.
- Olive green with canary yellow head and chest. Female and

immature: less yellow on nape.
- Usually seen in groups feeding in canopy.
- As it is confined to forest, not easily confused with Yellowhammer of open country.

Voice
- Loud trill and rattling call.

Food
- Feed mainly in canopy on insects, their larvae and spiders. Also take fruits.

Breeding
- Often polygamous.
- *Time:* November to December.
- *Nest:* Build nest similar to that of Whitehead but site it in a hole or cavity in tree.
- *Eggs:* 2 to 4 pinkish eggs with brown spots. Male does not appear to assist incubation of 20 or 21 days.

Distribution & Habitat
- Reasonable populations now only in Fiordland and Arthur's Pass National Park in South Island.
- Inhabits forest, mainly beech.

▼ **Yellowhead at nest hole.**

Brown Creeper/Pipipi
Mohoua novaeseelandiae

Family PACHYCEPHALIDAE
Genus *Mohoua*

Category
- Endemic.

Field Characteristics
- 13 cm.
- Generally light brown above and buff below.
- Very active and inquisitive.
- Seen in small flocks after nesting season.

Voice
- A rapid 'chi-chi-tee-tee'.

Food
- Insects and their larvae and spiders, also small fruits.

Breeding
- *Time:* Eggs laid from September to February.
- *Nest:* Built of leaves, mosses and lichens bound with cobweb, sited in dense shrub or manuka. Favourite site is in lawyer vine growing over matagouri.
- *Eggs:* Clutch of 2 to 4 cream-coloured eggs with dark-brown markings. Incubation by female for 17 days.
- *Chicks:* Fed by both parents.

Distribution & Habitat
- Widespread and common in South Island only.
- Inhabits native and exotic forests and scrub.

▼ **Brown Creeper.**

43 Grey Warbler/Riroriro
Gerygone igata

Family ACANTHIZIDAE
Genus *Gerygone*

Category
• Endemic. Closely related species in the Chatham Islands.

Field Characteristics
• 11 cm.
• Overall grey colour with white tip to tail in flight.
  Its small size, overall grey colour and continuous activity distinguish it from other species.
• Easily attracted to squeaker.
• Usually seen in pairs or small family groups.

Voice
• A melodious, wavering warble with song ended abruptly.
• Alarm note a repeated twitter.

◀ **Grey Warbler at nest.**
▼ **Grey Warbler and nest in kahikatea.**

Food
• Feeds entirely on insects and their larvae, and spiders.

Breeding
• *Time:* Three broods a year, commencing in August. Second brood in October often parasitised by Shining Cuckoo.
• *Nest:* Hanging nest built of moss, lichens, strips of bark and grasses, with dome and entrance at one side, and liberally lined with feathers.
• *Eggs:* Clutch of 3 or 4 pink eggs with brown spots is incubated by female for 18 days.

Distribution & Habitat
• Common throughout New Zealand.
• Inhabits native and exotic forests and scrub.

North Island Fantail/Piwakawaka
Rhipidura fuliginosa placabilis

South Island Fantail/Piwakawaka
Rhipidura fuliginosa fuliginosa

Family MONARCHIDAE
Genus *Rhipidura*

Category
- Native. Also in Australia and the Pacific.

Field Characteristics
- 16 cm. Smaller than House Sparrow. Chubby body, long tail often fanned.
- Two colour forms: the commonest form has creamy yellow undersides; the other is mostly black; the black form is more common in the South Island. Both have white ear patch, but not always present in black form.
- N.I. Fantail has half of each outer tail feather white; three-quarters of these feathers are white in S.I. Fantail.
- Constant activity.
- Often in pairs or family groups.

Voice
- Single sharp 'cheet' is contact call.
- Male has chattering song of several syllables.

Food
- Entirely insectivorous. Most insects caught on the wing.

- The fanned tail may act as sweep to disturb insects.
- Often flocks feed on grass paddocks in winter, sometimes landing on ground.

Breeding
- *Time:* From August to February, with 4 or 5 broods a year.
- *Nest:* Usually on slender branch or horizontal fork, often above water. Small, firm cup of fibres, moss, and bark, coated with spider web, with neat, fine fibre lining. Often has loose material hanging from base forming a beard.
- *Eggs:* Clutch of 2 or 3 cream-coloured eggs with brown spots. Incubated by both sexes for 15 days.

Distribution & Habitat
- Common throughout New Zealand. Black form of Fantail more common in South Island.
- Inhabits forests, scrub, suburban gardens and exotic pine forests.

◀ **North Island Fantail.**
◀ **Fantail nest in tanekaha.**

▲ Male North Island Tomtit at nest.

North Island Tomtit/Mirimiro
Petroica macrocephala toitoi

South Island Tomtit/Ngiru-ngiru
Petroica macrocephala macrocephala

Category
- Endemic.

Family EOPSALTRIIDAE
Genus *Petroica*

Field Characteristics
- 13 cm.
- Some South Island Tomtit males have yellow or orange breasts while others have white breasts, as in North Island sub-species. Both sexes have prominent white patch on wing, easily seen when in flight.
- Males are inquisitive and more often seen than the brownish-coloured females.

Voice
- Contact call is high-pitched 'tee-tee'. Male sings with a warbling 'yodi-yodi-yodi'.

Food
- Insects, their larvae, spiders and earthworms.

Breeding
- *Time:* August to January.
- *Nest:* Made of lichens, bark, moss and grasses bound with cobwebs. Built in tree cavities, ends of broken branches, under banks or in dead fronds on trunk of tree fern.
- *Eggs:* 3 to 5 cream-coloured eggs, brown markings. Incubated by female for 17 days.
- *Chicks:* Fed by both parents. After first brood is part grown, female builds second nest while male attends chicks.

Distribution & Habitat
- Forested areas and tall scrub throughout New Zealand.

◀ **Female North Island Tomtit at nest.**
▼ **Male South Island Tomtit.**

▼ **Immature female South Island Tomtit.**

North Island Robin/Toutouwai
Petroica australis longipes

South Island Robin/Toutouwai
Petroica australis australis

Stewart Island Robin
Petroica australis rakiura

Family EOPSALTRIIDAE
Genus *Petroica*

Category
• Endemic.

Field Characteristics
• 18 cm.
• North Island sub-species male is sooty black with white streaks on head and throat, white belly and undertail. Female is slightly browner above with light belly and undertail.
• South Island sub-species male is dusky black with cream-buff lower breast, belly and undertail cream. Female is slightly browner above.
• Stewart Island sub-species has white breast similar to that of N.I. sub-species.
• Noticeably long legs.
• Robins are confiding and approach humans to feed in areas of litter disturbed by feet.

Voice
• Song is a plaintive 'tweep-tweep' leading to a slow warble.

Sometimes sing without pause for up to an hour.

Food
• Insects, including large prey such as stick insects and wetas, grubs, spiders and earthworms.

Breeding
• *Time:* October to January.
• *Nest:* Bulky nest composed of leaves, small sticks, grasses and moss, is built in tree fork, hollow of tree or end of broken limb.
• *Eggs:* Clutch of 3 or 4 cream-coloured eggs with dark-brown spots. Double brooded. Female incubates for 18 to 20 days.
• *Chicks:* Fed by both sexes.

Distribution & Habitat
• Widely distributed in native and exotic forests and manuka scrub. Absent north of Te Aroha except for Little Barrier Island and Tiritiri Island.

◀ **South Island Robin.**
◀ **North Island Robin at nest.**

▲ Silvereyes.

Silvereye/Tauhou
Zosterops lateralis lateralis

Family ZOSTEROPIDAE
Genus *Zosterops*

Category
- Native. Self-introduced mid-1800s.
- Also South-eastern Australia.

Field Characteristics
- 12 cm. Much smaller body than House Sparrow.
- Bright yellowish green above with grey saddle, light grey breast and rusty flanks. Distinctive white eye ring.
- Usually seen in small groups moving rapidly through foliage. Visits garden bird-tables for bread, fruit and sugar-water.

Voice
- Contact call is sharp 'twee'.
- Male sings with subdued warbling trills.

◀ **Silvereye and nest.**
▼ **Silvereye.**

Food
- Insects, grubs, spiders, small fruits and nectar.
- Silvereyes also cause damage to orchard fruits.

Breeding
- *Time:* August to February, more than one clutch.
- *Nest:* Suspended from twigs of shrubs or bamboo. Flimsy and ladle-like, composed of fine grasses, hairs, moss and spider web.
- *Eggs:* Clutch of 2 or 3 pale-blue eggs, can often be seen through walls of nest. Incubation by both sexes for 12 days.

Distribution & Habitat
- Widespread throughout New Zealand.
- Common in native and exotic forests, scrub, orchards and suburban gardens.

▲ Female Bellbird at nest.

Bellbird/Makomako
Anthornis melanura melanura

Family MELIPHAGIDAE
Genus *Anthornis*

Category
- Endemic.

Field Characteristics
- 20 cm.
- Male has purple gloss on head and face. Female is duller, with narrow white stripe on cheek.
- Recognised by slight downcurve of bill and shallow fork in tail.

Voice
- Surprisingly loud voice in relation to size. Dawn song consists of 3 to 5 bell-like notes.
- Daytime song resembles that of Tui but notes are more pure and contain fewer guttural sounds.

Food
- Nectar, fruits, insects and spiders. Males take far more nectar than females. Latter take more insects.

Breeding
- *Time:* 2 broods a year are raised between September and January.
- *Nest:* Made of twigs, leaves and grasses built in shrub, fork of tree or in shallow tree cavity.
- *Eggs:* Clutch of 3 or 4 pinkish eggs with brown spots. Female incubates for 13 or 14 days.

Distribution & Habitat
- Common in native and exotic forests, orchards and gardens. Not common in Auckland or Northland, apart from Tiritiri Island, Whangaparoa Peninsula, and Shakespeare Reserve.
- Different sub-species inhabits Three Kings and Poor Knights Islands.

◀ **Bellbird, male.**
▼ **Male Bellbird singing.**

Tui
Prosthemadera novaeseelandiae novaeseelandiae

Family MELIPHAGIDAE
Genus *Prosthemadera*

Category
• Endemic.

Field Characteristics
• 30 cm. Males larger than females and immature birds.
• Conspicuous white throat feathers and white patch on wing. Dark brown middle back plumage, otherwise dark greenish black with metallic sheen.
• Downward curving beak.
• Strong, rapid, noisy flight.

Voice
• Song varies considerably with district. Bell-like notes, low whistles, chuckles and guttural 'squarks' are all part of repertoire.

Food
• Nectar, fruits and insects.

Often takes large insects such as stick insects. Fly considerable distances to feed on seasonal flowering plants, e.g. kowhai and pohutukawa.

Breeding
• *Time:* Eggs laid from September to January.
• *Nest:* Bulky nest of sticks, dry leaves and grasses is built in tree fork, shrub or manuka canopy.
• *Eggs:* Clutch of 2 or 3 pinkish eggs with light-brown spots. Incubated by female for 14 days.
• *Chicks:* Fed by both parents.

Distribution & Habitat
• Inhabits forests and forest remnants, orchards and gardens throughout New Zealand.

▼ Tuis at nest.

▼ Tui singing.

Index of Common Names

Index of Scientific Names